John Judson

Official program of exercised incident to dedication of the

Soldiers' and sailors' monument

John Judson

**Official program of exercised incident to dedication of the Soldiers' and sailors'
monument**

ISBN/EAN: 9783337134518

Printed in Europe, USA, Canada, Australia, Japan

Cover: Foto ©ninafisch / pixelio.de

More available books at **www.hansebooks.com**

HEADQUARTERS GRAND MARSHAL,

Soldiers' and Sailors' Monument Parade,

ROOM 17, CITY HALL.

NEW HAVEN, CONN, June 6th, 1887.

GENERAL ORDERS, No. 2.

I. Commanding Officers and Marshals of the various organizations parading in this city on the 17th of June next, will assemble their commands at the following points, in time to report the formation of their respective divisions to the Grand Marshal at 10.45 o'clock, A. M.

FIRST DIVISION.—MILITARY.

Brig. Gen'l Stephen R. Smith, Marshal.—On the north-east side of the Green, right resting on Elm Street.

SECOND DIVISION.

Brig. Gen'l Frank D. Sloat, Marshal.—Grand Army of the Republic; Naval Brigade and Battalion of Sons of Veterans, on Temple Street, right resting on Elm Street.

THIRD DIVISION.

Brig. Gen'l Erastus Blakeslee, Marshal.—Thirty-eight Barges containing young ladies from various Sunday Schools, representing the thirty-eight States of the Union, and Public School Memorial Guard.—On College Street, right resting on Elm Street.

FOURTH DIVISION.

Major C. W. Blakeslee, Jr., Marshal.—Uniformed Civic Societies; Knights of Pythias, Sarsfield Zouaves, Improved Order of Red Men, and others.—On High Street, between Elm and Wall Streets, right resting on Elm Street.

FIFTH DIVISION.

Charles Weidig, Marshal.—German Societies, Turner Society, Arion Singing Society, Harugari Singing Society, Tentonia Singing Society, Cecilia Singing Society, Bavarian Society, Hessen Society, Schwaben Society, Plattdeutsche Society, Viking Swedish Society.—On York Street, between Elm and Grove Streets, right resting on Elm street.

SIXTH DIVISION.

Major William A. Lincoln, Marshal.—Volunteer Veteran Firemen's Association, Civic Societies, Knights of Columbus, Catholic Temperance Societies, Patriotic Sons of America, Italian Associations, Garibaldi Society, and other civic societies.—On York Street, between Elm and Chapel Streets, right resting on Elm Street.

SEVENTH DIVISION.

Colonel A. C. Hendrick, (Chief) Marshal. — Fire Department of New Haven.—On Church Street, right resting on Elm Street.

FIRST SECTION OF CARRIAGES.

General George H. Ford, Assistant Marshal.—Carriages containing the Governor and Staff, United States Senators and Representatives, State Officers, President of the Day, Orator of the Day, Chaplain of the Day, and Monument Committee,—will assemble on Temple Street, on the Green, right resting on Elm Street.

SECOND SECTION OF CARRIAGES.

Captain E. A. Gessner, S. M. Crampton, G. E. Osborn, D. N. Moore, E. Hewett, M. F. Campbell, C. E. Hoadley, Assistant Marshals.—Carriages containing distinguished Military Guests, Mexican Veterans, etc.—will form on Temple Street, on the left of first section.

THIRD SECTION OF CARRIAGES.

Capt. Chas. E. Rounds, H. S. Holcomb, E. F. Mansfield. Capt. S. E. Chaffe, Assistant Marshals.—Carriages containing distinguished Naval Officers, will form on Temple Street, on the left of second section.

FOURTH SECTION OF CARRIAGES.

L. D. Chidsey, Wm. F. Sternburg, F. H. Benton, Capt. A. E. Beardsley, Assistant Marshals.—Carriages containing the Mayor of New Haven and visiting Mayors of other cities, Town Agent, and Selectmen of New Haven, visiting

Selectmen, Board of Aldermen and Common Council, ex-Governors, Judges of United States and State Courts, and other invited guests, will form on College Street, between Elm and Chapel Streets, right resting on Elm Street.

II.—The procession will move promptly at 11.00 o'clock A. M. Three strokes upon Centre Church bell will be given as a signal for the first division to move. The line of march will be through the following streets:—Up Elm to Howe, Howe to Chapel, Chapel to Orange, through Orange Street to Farnam Drive, Farnam Drive to the Monument in East Rock Park.

III.—When the head of the column arrives at York and Chapel Streets, the first division will halt and form in line, face to the front, dress to the right and prepare to receive the reviewing officers. The reviewing officers will then pass the line to the reviewing stand in front of the Hyperion. Having taken their position, the entire line will break into column of companies and pass in review. When the left of the column has passed the reviewing officers, the column will again halt, form in line and the reviewing officers, escorted by the Grand Marshal and Staff, will pass the line to their respective positions in the column, when the column will again take up the line of march for its destination.

IV.—When the third division arrives at the English Drive they will proceed up English Drive to the position assigned them at the monument.

V.—Upon arrival at the monument the first and second divisions will pass around the monument to the left and return down Farnam Drive to a point opposite the

Whitneyville road, to the refreshment tents, where a collation will be provided.

VI.—After refreshments have been served and the necessary rest taken, the first and second divisions, except the Governor's Foot and Horse Guards, will return via Farnam Drive to Orange Street, Orange to Trumbull, Trumbull to State, State to Olive, Olive to Chapel, Chapel Street to the Green, where they will be dismissed.

VII.—The third, fourth, fifth and sixth divisions will remain at the monument during the dedication ceremonies and at the close return in a body via English Drive, over the same route as specified in section VI, and be dismissed at the Green.

VIII.—The seventh division (Fire Department), will not enter the Park, but will be dismissed at the Orange Street bridge.

IX.—The Governor's Foot and Horse Guards will return to the monument after being served with refreshments, and perform escort duty to the Governor and other guests, passing down English Drive to Orange Street, Orange to Trumbull, Trumbull to Temple, Temple to Chapel, Chapel Street to the Hyperion, where they will be dismissed.

X.—On the morning of the 17th inst. the Headquarters of the Grand Marshal will be established at the State House, north entrance, from 9.00 to 10.30 o'clock A. M.

XI.—The General Staff and Aids will report for duty at 9.00 o'clock A. M. Assistant Marshals not previously assigned to duty will report to General George M. Harmon, Chief of Staff, who will assign them a position in line. At 10.30 o'clock A. M. the Grand Marshal and Staff will take position at the right of the line on Elm Street, between Temple and College Streets, left resting on Temple Street. The success of the parade depends largely upon the promptness and regularity with which the column moves. And the announcement is made that the column will move precisely at the hour named. It is expected that Marshals of Divisions will be prepared to move their commands promptly on time.

By order of GENERAL EDWIN S. GREELEY,

Grand Marshal.

JOHN G. HEALY,

OFFICIAL: Lt.-Col and Adjt.-General.

FRED H. WALDRON,

Capt. and Asst. Adjt.-General.

Headquarters Grand Marshal,

Soldiers' and Sailors' Monument Parade,

ROOM 17, CITY HALL.

New Haven, Conn., June 10th, 1887.

General Orders, No. 3.

The several divisions parading in this city on the 17th inst., on the occasion of the dedication of the Soldiers' and Sailors' Monument, will be formed in the following

ORDER OF PROCESSION.

PLATOON OF POLICE.

Fifth Regiment Artillery Band, U. S. A.
Daniel Wiegand, Band Master.

GRAND MARSHAL.

Brevet-Brigadier-General Edwin S. Greeley, U. S.
Vols., Colonel Tenth Conn. Vols.

11

GENERAL STAFF.

Brigadier-General George M. Harmon, First Connecticut Volunteer Artillery, Chief of Staff.

Lieutenant Colonel John G. Healy, Ninth Connecticut Volunteers, Adjutant General.

Captain Fred. H. Waldron, First Connecticut Volunteer Artillery, Assistant Adjutant General.

Brigadier-General John L. Otis, Tenth Connecticut Volunteers.

Colonel A. L. Gurney, Second New York Cavalry.

Colonel J. W. Knowlton, Fourteenth Connecticut Volunteers.

Lieutenant Colonel Francis Bacon, Surgeon United States Volunteers.

Major A. T. Douglass, Surgeon Tenth Connecticut Volunteers.

Major B. H. Cheney, Assistant Staff Surgeon Fourth Army Corps.

Rev. H. Clay Trumbull, Chaplain Tenth Connecticut Volunteers, Chaplain-in-Chief M. O. L. L. of the United States.

AIDS.

Major Charles A. Brooks, Ninth Maine Volunteers.

Major Patrick Maher, Twenty-fourth Connecticut Volunteers.

Major John E. Clark, Fifth Michigan Cavalry. Troop

Major T. Attwater Barnes, Ex-Brigade Inspector Connecticut National Guard.

Captain William H. Pierpont, Seventh Connecticut Volunteers.

Captain Charles E. Hart, One Hundred and Ninth United States C. T.

Captain Alfred B. Beers, Sixth Connecticut Volunteers.

Captain Samuel Bolton, Twenty-second Regt., N. G., S. N. Y.

Lieutenant Frank A Munson, First New York Cavalry.

Sergeant Allen D. Baldwin, Twenty-seventh Connecticut Volunteers.

Sergeant E. S. Wheeler, Q. M. Sergeant Twenty-first Connecticut Volunteers

Bernard E. Lynch.	E. G. Stoddard.
Eli Whitney, Jr.	W. H. Carmalt, M. D.
Henry W. Farnam.	Thomas Hooker.
Samuel T. Dutton.	W. H. Brown.

Orderly, David Chadeayne, Tenth Connecticut Volunteers.

FIRST DIVISION.

MILITARY.

MARSHAL.

BRIGADIER-GENERAL STEPHEN R. SMITH.

ASSISTANT MARSHALS.

Gen. Frederick Barton, New Haven, Commissary General ex-Governor Harrison's Staff.

Gen. Henry P. Geib, Stamford, Surgeon General ex-Governor Harrison's Staff.

Gen. George H. Ford, New Haven, Commissary General ex-Governor Bigelow's Staff.

Gen. W. W. Skiddy, Stamford, Commissary General Ex-Governor Waller's Staff.

Col. William C. Mowry, Norwich, Aide-de-Camp ex-Governor Harrison's Staff.

Col. Wm. E. Hyde, Danielsonville, Aide-de-Camp ex-Governor Harrison's Staff.

Col. Tracy B. Warren, Bridgeport, Aide-de-Camp ex-Governor Harrison's Staff.

Col. Norris G, Osborn, New Haven, Aide-de-Camp ex Governor Waller's Staff.

Col. Wm. H. Stevenson, Bridgeport, Aide-de-Camp ex-Governor Waller's Staff.

Col. Frank L. Bigelow, New Haven, Aide-de-Camp ex-Governor Bigelow's Staff.

Major Charles E. Doty, South Norwalk, Ex-Brigade Quartermaster.

Major Fred A. Spencer, Waterbury, ex-Brigade Inspector of Rifle Practice.

Major James E. Stetson, New Haven, ex-Brigade Inspector of Rifle Practice.

Major Samuel C. Waldron, East Providence, R. I., Ex-Brigade Commissary.

Major Clarence S. Steele, Quartermaster First Brigade New Jersey National Guard.

Capt. Newell A. Thompson, Boston, Aide-de-Camp and Acting Assistant Inspector General Second Brigade, Mass. Vol. Militia, and Adjutant Ancient and Honorable Artillery Co., Massachusetts.

Lieut. Charles E. Granniss, New Haven, ex-First Lieutenant Co. F. Second Regiment, C. N. G.

13

BRIGADE. CONNECTICUT NATIONAL GUARD.

Headquarters, Middletown.

BRIG. GEN. CHARLES P. GRAHAM, Middletown, Commanding.

BRIGADE STAFF.

Lieut. Col. Joseph T. Elliott, Assistant Adjutant General, Middletown.
Major Alexander Allen, Brigade Inspector, Hartford.
Major Edward S. Hayden, Brigade Quartermaster, Waterbury.
Major Walter M. Wellman, Brigade Commissary, New Haven.
Major Samuel J. Miller, Brigade Inspector of Rifle Practice, Willimantic.
Lieutenant Colonel C. Purdy Lindsley, Medical Director, New Haven.
Major Charles L. Burdett, Engineer and Signal Officer, Hartford.
Captain William H. Stratton, Aide-de-Camp, New Haven.
Captain Charles G. Lyon, Aid-de-Camp, Bridgeport.
Sergeant John Bartholomew, Orderly, Guilford.
Sergeant Merritt W. Burwell, Orderly, New Haven.
Sergeant Russell H. Whitaker, Brigade Trumpeter, Middletown.

FOURTH REGIMENT.

Headquarters, Bridgeport.

Fourth Regiment Band (Wheeler & Wilson's), Bridgeport, S. C. Rosenberg, Chief Musician.
Regimental Drum and Trumpet Corps.
Regimental Signal Corps.

FIELD AND STAFF.

COLONEL THOMAS L. WATSON, Bridgeport, Commanding Regiment.

Lieutenant Colonel, Henry Skinner, West Winsted.
Major, James C. Crowe, South Norwalk.
Adjutant, Captain Louis N. VanKeuren, Bridgeport.
Quartermaster, 1st Lieutenant Howard G. Hubbell, Bridgeport.
Paymaster, 1st Lieutenant George S. Rowe, West Winsted.
Surgeon, Major George L. Porter, Bridgeport.
Assistant Surgeon, 1st Lieutenant Charles S. Murray, Norwalk.
Inspector of Rifle Practice, Captain Samuel C. Kingman, Bridgeport.
Signal Officer, 1st Lieutenant William W. Starr, Jr., Bridgeport.
Chaplain, Rev. Robert G. S. McNeille, Bridgeport.

COMPANY F, Norwalk, Capt. Addison A Betts.
1st Lieut. Harvey M. Kent ; 2d Lieut. Henry Matheis.
COMPANY C, Stamford, Capt. William F. Daniel.
1st Lieut. William B. Cochrane ; 2d Lieut. Harry N. Covell
COMPANY D, South Norwalk, Capt. Russell Frost.
1st Lieut. Cornelius Elwood; 2d Lieut. John McGraw.
COMPANY E, Bridgeport, Capt. James Sheridan.
1st Lieut. James Donnelly; 2d Lieut. John J. Glennon.
COMPANY I, West Winsted, Capt. Edward Finn.
1st Lieut. George E. Wright; 2d Lieut. Michael J. Finn.
COMPANY K, Stratford, Capt. Eugene Morehouse.
1st Lieut. Stiles Judson, Jr.; 2d Lieut. George T. Jewell.
COMPANY G, Danbury, Capt. Frank R. Nash.
1st Lieut. George L. Stevens; 2d Lieut. William Phillips.
COMPANY B, Bridgeport, Capt. George W. Cornell.
1st Lieut. Charles H. Gibner; 2d Lieut. Garrie P. Sanger.

NON-COMMISSIONED STAFF.

Sergeant Major, George E. Derrick, Bridgeport.
Quarter-Master Sergeant, Frederick S. Beardsley, Stratford.
Commissary Sergeant, James A. Morris, Bridgeport.
Hospital Steward, Fred. S. Stevens, Bridgeport.
Chief Trumpeter, John Brown.
Drum Major, William Flynn, Bridgeport.

FOURTH MACHINE-GUN PLATOON.

(Gatling Gun) Bridgeport, 2d Lieut. Edwin F. Hall, Commanding.

15

FIRST REGIMENT.

Headquarters, Hartford.

First Regiment Band, (Colt's,) Hartford, Fred. J. Walker, Leader.
Regimental Drum and Trumpet Corps.
Regimental Signal Corps.

FIELD AND STAFF.

COLONEL WILLIAM E. CONE, Hartford, Commanding Regiment.

Lieutenant Colonel Charles E. Thompson, Hartford.
Major Thomas M. Smith, Hartford.
Adjutant, Captain Phineas H. Ingalls, Hartford.
Quartermaster, 1st Lieutenant Theron C. Swan, Hartford.
Paymaster, 1st Lieutenant Wallace T. Fenn, Hartford.
Surgeon, Major Harmon G. Howe, Hartford.
Assistant Surgeon, 1st Lieutenant Henry S. Otis, Hartford.
Inspector of Rifle Practice, Captain James B. Houston, Enfield.
Signal Officer, 1st Lieutenant Morris Penrose, Hartford.
Chaplain, Rev. James W. Cooper, New Britain.
COMPANY D, New Britain, Capt. Augustus N. Bennett.
1st Lieut. William E. Allen ; 2d Lieut. John McBriarty.
COMPANY K, Hartford, Capt. Samuel O. Prentice.
1st Lieut. James H. Jarman ; 2d Lieut. DeWitt P. Preston.
COMPANY F, Hartford, Capt. George B. Newton.
1st Lieut. Everett L. Morse ; 2d Lieut. Louis B. Hubbard.
COMPANY H, Hartford, Capt. Wm. H. McLean.
1st Lieut. Henry E. Chapman ; 2d Lieut. Charles H. Patterson.
COMPANY A, Hartford, Capt. Edward Schulze.
1st Lieut. Henry F. Smith ; 2d Lieut. George Senk.
COMPANY G, South Manchester, Capt. John Hickey.
1st Lieut. Charles L. Bissell ; 2d Lieut. —— ————
COMPANY B, Hartford, Capt. Thomas F. Flanigan.
1st Lieut. Patrick H. Smith ; 2d Lieut. John J. Leahy.
COMPANY E, New Britain, Capt. Alfred L. Thompson.
1st Lieut. John J. Smith ; 2d Lieut. Henry G. Upson.

NON-COMMISSIONED STAFF.

Sergeant Major, Alfred W. Green, Hartford.
Quarter-Master Sergeant, Elmer C. Quiggle, Hartford.
Commissary Sergeant, Clarence H. Wickham, Hartford.
Hospital Steward, Charles E. Goodrich, Hartford.
Chief Trumpeter, Henry Scheuy, New Britain.
Drum Major, William C. Steele, Hartford.

FIRST MACHINE-GUN PLATOON.

(Gatling Gun) Hartford, 2d Lieut. Henry Avery, Commanding.

SECOND REGIMENT.

Headquarters, New Haven.

Second Regiment Band (American), New Haven.
George Streit, Chief Musician.
Regimental Drum and Trumpet Corps.
Regimental Signal Corps.

FIELD AND STAFF.

COLONEL WALTER J. LEAVENWORTH, Wallingford, Commanding Regiment.

Lieutenant Colonel, John B. Doherty, Waterbury.
Major, Frank T. Lee, New Haven.
Adjutant, Captain Thomas T. Welles, New Haven.
Quartermaster, 1st Lieutenant Francis J. Duffy, New Haven.
Paymaster, 1st Lieutenant William H. Newton, Wallingford.
Surgeon, Major Evelyn L. Bissell, New Haven.
Assistant Surgeon, 1st Lieutenant Carl E. Munger, Waterbury.
Inspector of Rifle Practice, Captain Andrew Allen, New Haven.
Signal Officer, 1st Lieutenant William E. Jackson, New Haven.
Chaplain, (vacant.)

COMPANY I, Meriden, Capt. Henry B. Wood.
　　　　1st Lieut. Charles B. Bowen; 2d Lieut. Frederick T. Ward.
COMPANY C, New Haven, Capt. John Garrity.
　　　　1st Lieut. Timothy F. Callahan; 2d Lieut. Michael Creed.

COMPANY E, New Haven. Capt. Theodore H. Sucher.
　　　　　1st Lieut. Robert M. Walker; 2d Lieut. Leverett B. Fairchild.
COMPANY G, Waterbury, Capt. Alfred J. Wolff.
　　　　　1st Lieut. Kyron J. Farrell; 2d Lieut. Daniel E. Fitzpatrick.
COMPANY D, New Haven, Capt. Andrew H. Embler,
　　　　　1st Lieut. Robert G. Christie; 2d Lieut. Edward I. Williams.
COMPANY A, Waterbury, Capt. ——— ———
　　　　　1st Lieut. Lucien F. Barpee; 2d Lieut. Frank M. Bronson.
COMPANY H, Middletown, Capt. Wesley U. Pearne.
　　　　　1st Lieut. Benjamin D. Putnam; 2d Lieut. Nathan H. Smith.
COMPANY F, New Haven, Capt. Charles C. Ford.
　　　　　1st Lieut. Harvey S. Munson; 2d Lieut. John T. Gill.
COMPANY B, New Haven, Capt. John Gutt.
　　　　　1st Lieut. Charles G. Miller; 2d Lieut. George M. Schaffuer.
COMPANY K, Wallingford, Capt. Bryant A. Treat.
　　　　　1st Lieut. George G. La Barnes; 2d Lieut. ——— ———

NON-COMMISSIONED STAFF.

Sergeant Major, Francis B. Lane, New Haven.
Quartermaster Sergeant, Ithiel W. Doolittle, New Haven.
Commissary Sergeant, Henry P. Viberts, Jr., Meriden.
Hospital Steward, Ellsworth S. Scofield, New Haven.
Chief Trumpeter, James M. Hennessey, New Haven.
Drum Major, Albert 'F'. Sawe, West Haven.

SECOND MACHINE GUN PLATOON.

(Gatling Gun) New Haven, 2d Lieut. William H. Sears, Commanding.

————

THIRD REGIMENT.

Headquarters, New London.

Third Regiment Band, New London.
Edward A. Colby, Chief Musician.
Regimental Drum and Trumpet Corps.
Regimental Signal Corps.

FIELD AND STAFF.

COLONEL GEORGE HAVEN, New London, Commanding Regiment.

Lieutenant-Colonel, Michael Twomey, Pawcatuck.
Major, William F. Bidwell, Norwich.
Adjutant, Captain Hezekiah B. Smith, New London.
Quartermaster, First Lieutenant William E. Pendleton, New London.
Paymaster, First Lieutenant George M. Cole, New London.
Surgeon, Major Leonard B. Almy, Norwich.
Assistant Surgeon, First Lieutenant H. L. Hammond, Killingly.
Inspector of Rifle Practice, Captain J. E. Harris, New London.
Signal officer, First Lieutenant Thomas H. Allen, Sprague.
Chaplain, Rev. Nicholas T. Allen, Groton.

COMPANY I, New London, Captain Abner N. Sterry; 1st Lieut., Frank P. Goff; 2d Lieut., Samuel Prince.

COMPANY E. Willimantic, Capt. Patrick Fitzpatrick; 1st Lieut., Thomas Ashton; 2d Lieut., John H. Morrison.

COMPANY C, Norwich, Capt. Thomas B. Linton; 1st Lieutenant,' Irving E. Hill; 2d Lieut., Fred A. Fox.

COMPANY G, Putnam, Capt. Clinton A. Winslow, 1st Lieutenant, Edward G. Wright; 2d Lieut., Alfred M. Parker.

COMPANY F, Danielsonville, Capt. Paul L. Gibson; 1st Lieut., John Armstrong; 2d Lieutenant, Kent A. Darbie.

COMPANY A. New London, Capt. —— —— —— 1st Lieutenant, John F. Murray, 2d Lieut., Edward R. May.

COMPANY B, Pawcatuck. Capt. Daniel Keleher; 1st Lieut., Cornelius Bransfield; 2d Lieut., Edmund Keleher.

COMPANY D, New London, Capt. Frederick E. St. Clare; 1st Lieutenant, William M. Mason; 2d Lieut., Michael J. Roach.

NON-COMMISSIONED STAFF.

Sergeant Major, David Conner, New London.
Quartermaster Sergeant, Charles F. Holt, New London.
Commissary Sergeant, Gilbert C. Bishop, New London.
Hospital Steward, William S. Starr, New London.
Chief Trumpeter, George L. Holmes, New London.
Drum Major, Benjamin M. Carroll, New London.

THIRD MACHINE GUN PLATOON.

(Gatling Gun) New London, 2d Lieutenant Charles F. Chaney, Commanding.

FIFTH BATTALION.

Battalion Drum and Trumpet Corps.
Battalion Signal Corps.

FIELD AND STAFF.

MAJOR FRANK M. WELCH, Bridgeport, Commanding Battalion.

Adjutant, Capt. Charles S. Tatten, Bridgeport.
Quartermaster, 1st Lieutenant, William P. H. Cross, Hartford.
Assistant Surgeon, 1st Lieutenant, William H. Donaldson, Fairfield.

COMPANY B, Hartford, Capt. Lloyd G. Seymour; 1st Lieut., L. Eugene
Seymour; 2d Lieut., John Jones.
COMPANY A, New Haven, Capt. Daniel S. Lathrop; 1st Lieut., Daniel Tilgh
man; 2d Lieut., Charles E. Fuller.
COMPANY C, Bridgeport, Capt. Charles H. Walker; 1st Lieutenant, Samuel
J. Benedict; 2d Lieut., William H. Latimer.

NON-COMMISSIONED STAFF.

Sergeant Major, J. Andrew Bell, New Haven.
Quartermaster Sergeant, James A. Taylor, Bridgeport.
Signal Sergeant, George Salisbury, New Haven.
Chief Trumpeter, Richmond L. Hazzard, Westville.
Drum Major, John D. Cowes, New Haven.

BATTERY A, LIGHT ARTILLERY.

Headquarters, Guilford.

CAPTAIN ARTHUR S. FOWLER, Guilford, Commanding Battery.

NON-COMMISSIONED STAFF.

First Sergeant, Thomas H. Matthews, New Haven.
Quartermaster Sergeant, Frank A. Morse, Guilford.
Veterinary Sergeant, James Smith, East Haven.
Guidon, William J. Howd, Stony Creek.

SECOND PLATOON, BRANFORD.

1st Lieut. James T. Reynolds; 2d Lieut. James H. Barker.

FIRST PLATOON, GUILFORD.

1st Lieut. William H. Lee ; 2d Lieut. Nelson S. Leete,

PUTNAM PHALANX.

Putnam Phalanx Drum Corps, Norman L. Hope, Drum Major.

Putnam Phalanx, of Hartford, Major Joseph Warner, Commanding.

STAFF.

Adjutant, Charles A. Lord.
Secretary, R. S. Peck.
Chief of Staff, Theodore Colston.
Quartermaster and Treasurer, O. H. Blanchard.
Inspector, Dudley Fox.
Historian, F. M. Brown.
Judge Advocate, C. H. Clark.
Paymaster, Henry Kennedy.
Surgeon, N. W. Holcombe, M. D.
Chaplain, Rev. W. L. Gage.
Engineer, B. C. Porter.
Commissary, Thomas Dowd.
Sergeant Major, Theodore I. Pease.

FIRST COMPANY, Capt. E. A. Perry.
　　　　　1st Lieut. A. B. Stockwell; 2d Lieut. H. B. Philbrick;
　　　　　Ensign John S. Russell.
SECOND COMPANY, Capt. Lyman Smith.
　　　　　1st Lieut. George H. Woolley, 2d Lieut. C. F. Hurd
　　　　　Ensign J. N. Shedd.
VETERAN CORPS, Capt. J. H. Welch, M. D.
　　　　　1st Lieut. A. R. Goodrich; 2d Lieut. T. A. Honiss;
　　　　　Ensign G. S. Catlin.

21

EMERALD GUARD.

New Haven.

Drum Corps.

Captain J. Francis Baker, Commanding.

1st Lieut., D. Flynn.   2d Lieut, John Kelly.

BATTALION GOV'S FOOT GUARDS.

Major John C. Kinney, Hartford, Commanding Battalion.

Weed's Band, of Hartford, Prof. John P. King, Leader.

Second Company Governor's Foot Guards, of New Haven.

(Chartered 1775.)

Captain, Edward J. Morse,

1st Lieut., Albert M. Johnson,   2d Lieut. Joseph J. Wooster.

Allen's Drum Corps, Hartford.

First Company Governor's Foot Guards, Hartford.

(Chartered 1771.)

Major, John C. Kinney.   Capt. James C. Pratt.
Lieut. and Adjt. J. Robert Dwyer.   Lieut. Theodore C. Nædle.
Lieut. Fayette C. Clark.   Ensign, Horace G. Lord.

STAFF.

Paymaster, Charles C. Strong,   Surgeon, Dr. M. M. Johnson,
Quartermaster, Linus T. Fenn,   Assistant Surgeon, Dr. W.A. M. Wainwright,
Commissary, Leander Hall,   Judge Advocate, E. H. Hyde,
Chaplain, James W. Bradin,   Engineer, George H. Folts,
              Inspector Rifle Practice, J. J. Poole.

IN CARRIAGES.

His Excellency, Phineas C. Lounsbury. Ridgefield, Governor and Commander-in-Chief.

STAFF.

Adjutant-General, Brig. Gen. Frederick E. Camp, Middletown.
Quartermaster-General, Brig. Gen. Charles Olmstead, Norwalk.
Surgeon-General, Brig. Gen. Charles J. Fox, Windham.
Commissary-General, Brig. Gen. John B. Clapp, Hartford.
Paymaster-General, Brig. Gen. Charles H. Pine, Derby.
Aide-de-Camp, Col. Samuel B. Horne, Winchester.
Aide-de-Camp, Col. Selah G. Blakeman, Huntington.
Aide-de-Camp, Col. J. Dwight Chaffee, Mansfield.
Aide-de-Camp, Col. Elwin H. Mathewson, Norwalk.
Assistant Adjutant-General, Col. George M. White, New Haven.
Assistant Quartermaster-General, Lieut. Col. Henry C. Morgan, Colchester.
Executive Secretary, George P. McLean, Simsbury.

MONUMENT COMMITTEE.

Gen. Samuel E. Merwin, chairman.

Ex-Gov. James E. English.
Ex-Gov. Hobart B. Bigelow.
Ex-Gov. Henry B. Harrison.
Hon. James Reynolds.
Theodore A. Tuttle.
Gen. Frank D. Sloat.

Hon. Joseph D. Plunkett.
John McCarthy.
Lieut. Col. John G. Healy.
Conrad Hofacker.
Lieut. Col. Samuel Tolles.
  Col. Simeon J. Fox, Secretary.

Rev. Timothy Dwight, D. D.; L. L. D., Pres't Yale College, Pres't of the Day
Rev. Newman Smyth, D. D., Orator of the Day.
Rev. Edwin Harwood, D. D., Chaplain of the Day.

CONNECTICUT REPRESENTATIVES IN CONGRESS.

Hon. Orville H. Platt, Meriden, United States Senator.
Gen. Joseph R. Hawley, Hartford, United States Senator.
Representative 1st District, Hon. Robert J. Vance, New Britain.
Representative 2d District, Hon. Carlos French, Seymour.
Representative 3d District, Hon. Chas. A. Russell, Killingly.
Representative 4th District, Hon. Miles T. Granger, North Canaan.

STATE OFFICERS.

Lieutenant Governor, James L. Howard, Hartford.
Secretary of State, Leverett M. Hubbard, Wallingford.
Treasurer, Alexander Warner, Pomfret.
Comptroller, Thomas Clark, Stonington.

BATTALION GOV'S HORSE GUARDS.

Major Horace H. Strong, Commanding Battalion.

National Band, of Wallingford, David McDonald, Leader.

Second Company Governor's Horse Guards, of New Haven.

(Chartered 1808).

Major, Horace H. Strong.
Captain, W. H. Farnham, Jr.
First Lieutenants, W. Burr Hall, D. A. Blakeslee.
Second Lieutenants, E. A. Todd; Luzerne Ludington.
Cornet, F. L. Newton.
Quartermaster, Isaac W. Hine.

Griswold Band (mounted), Hartford, Elmer E. Griswold, Leader.

First Company Governor's Horse Guards, of Hartford.

(Chartered 1778).

Major, Frank Cowles.
Captain, Charles O. Purinton.
Lieutenant, William G. Hubbard.
Cornet, Charles H. Dillings.
Quartermaster, Joseph C. McClure.
Secretary, F. M. Warren.

SECOND DIVISION.

VETERANS.

Brigadier General F. D. Sloat, Marshal.

ASSISTANT MARSHALS.

Adjutant G. F. Peterson, Twenty-seventh Connecticut Volunteers.

Lieutenant W. H. Stowe, Sixth Connecticut Volunteers.

Captain E. C. Dow, First Connecticut Volunteer Artillery.

Captain D. S. Thomas, Twenty-seventh Connecticut Volunteers.

Lieutenant David C. Monson, Second Connecticut Volunteer Artillery.

S. S. Thompson, Twenty-seventh Connecticut Volunteers.

T. E. Twitchell, Twelfth Connecticut Volunteers.

C. T. Ward, First Connecticut Volunteer Artillery.

O. 1. Woodford, Eleventh Connecticut Volunteers.

Lieutenant E. E. Stevens, Quartermaster Seventh Connecticut Volunteers.

H. W. Clark, Twenty-seventh Connecticut Volunteers.

Lieutenant G. H. Dayton, First Connecticut Volunteer Artillery.

L. E. Peck, Seventh Connecticut Volunteers.

Captain F. M. Bunce, United States Navy.

A. J. Ewen, Sons of Veterans.

Rockville Band, D. E. Brainard, Leader.

DEPARTMENT OF CONN., G. A. R.

Commander, Henry E. Taintor, Hartford.

S. V. Commander, Samuel B. Horne, Winsted.
J. V. Commander, William H. Pierpont, New Haven.
Medical Director, Henry P. Geib, Stamford.
Chaplain, Rev. Edward Anderson, Norwalk.
Assistant Adjutant-General, John H. Thacher, Hartford.
Assistant Quartermaster-General, William E. Morgan, New Haven.
Inspector, Daniel S. Kiefer, Waterbury.
Judge-Advocate, Edwin O. Dimock, Rockville.
Chief Mustering Officer, W. H. Tubbs, New London.
POST 1—Sedgwick, Norwich, J. Herbert George, Commander.
Hartford City Drum Corps.
2—Nathaniel Lyon, Hartford, G. R. Hurlbert, Commander.
Drum Corps.
3—Elias Howe, Jr., Bridgeport, Thomas Boudren, Commander.
5—Edward A. Doolittle, Cheshire, Jesse H. Rice, Commander.
7—Mason Rogers, Branford, E. C. Johnson, Commander.
Fife and Drum Corps.
8—Merriam, Meriden, A. F. Hall, Commander.
11—Stanley, New Britain, Patrick Marr, Commander.
13—Gilbert W. Thompson, Bristol, George Merriam, Jr., Commander.
Drum Corps.
14—Upton, New Milford, D. E. Soule, Commander.
Southington Band, twenty pieces.
16—Trumbull, Southington, F. A. Sutliff, Commander.
American Band, Providence, D. W. Reeves, Leader.
17—Admiral Foote, New Haven, James N. Coe, Commander.

IN CARRIAGES.

General W. T. Sherman.
General Philip H. Sheridan.
Aide-de-Camp Colonel Sanford C. Kellogg.
General John M. Schofield.
General Alfred H. Terry.

General A. W. Greely.
General Lucius Fairchild, Commander-in-Chief G. A. R. and Staff.
General William B. Franklin.
General D. N. Couch.
General Daniel E. Sickles.
General Edward Harland.
General J. A. Johnson.
General H. B. Carrington. _
General Dwight Morris.
General Edward L. Molineux.
General A. P. Rockwell.
Colonel Albermarle Cady.
Colonel William B. Wooster.
General William H. Noble.
General L. A. Dickinson.
General L. W. Wessels.
General William H. Bulkeley.
Colonel George L. Febiger.
Colonel Fred. D. Grant.
Colonel Frank W. Cheney.
Major Lyman Bissell.
Major George C. Jarvis.
Major M. T. Newton.
Major John A. Tibbets.
Major O. R. Fyler.
And other Military Officers.

Veteran C. H. Frisbie riding horse that was in seventeen engagements in army of the Potomac, and carries three rebel bullets in his body.

Drum Corps.
POST 52—Henry C. Merwin, New Haven, Ralph Wright, Commander.
76—Gen. Von Steinwehr, New Haven, Joseph Schleicher, Commander.
Band.
23—Hobbie, Stamford, George W. Sinclair, Commander.
24—Lombard, Greenwich, John E. Foster, Commander.
Chester Drum Corps.
25—Mather, Deep River, Walter S. Clark, Commander.
26—Kellogg, Birmingham, Samuel Miller, Commander.
Austin Drum Corps.
33—Palmer, West Winsted, George L. Andrews, Commander.
36—Arthur H. Dutton, Wallingford, Ira B. Smith, Commander.
Echo Drum Corps.
39—George Van Horn, Milford, W. S. Chase, Commander.

40—Upson, Seymour, Robert Healy, Commander.
42—Parmellee, Guilford, Hart Landon, Commander.
Drum Corps.
47—W. W. Perkins, New London, H. B. Smith, Commander.
48—Douglas Fowler, South Norwalk, W. A. Hendrick, Commander.
Mattatuck Drum Corps.
49—Wadhams, Waterbury, John M. Gallagher, Commander.
Drum Corps.
50—Robert O. Tyler, Hartford, Horace R. Morley, Commander.
Mansfield Post Drum Corps.
53—Mansfield, Middletown, Edwin Bywater, Commander.
56—Samuel Brown, Thompsonville, Andrew Gordon, Commander.
Plainville Drum Corps.
57—Newton S. Manross, Forestville, Charles W. Brown, Commander.
60—David S. Cowles, Canaan, Edward S. Roberts, Commander.
63—Harry McDonough, Westport, John P. Perry, Commander.
65—Daniel C. Rodman, East Hartford, D. C. Clark, Commander.
66—John M. Morris, Wethersfield, Stephen Morgan, Commander.
West Hartford Drum Corps.
67—J. H. Converse, Windsor Locks, A. W. Converse, Commander.
69—P. M. Trowbridge, Woodbury, Henry F. Gibson, Commander.
72—Chapman, Westbrook, Z. E. Morgan, Commander.
Farrell's Advance Drum Corps.
75—Thomas M. Renshaw, Ansonia, J. A. Bristol, Commander.
Hancock Post Drum Corps.
81—Hancock, Pawcatuck, Charles H. Browning, Commander.
82—J. F. Trumbull, Stonington, J. S. Anderson, Commander.
Disabled Veterans in Barges.

UNITED STATES NAVAL BRIGADE.

William S. Wells, Second Assistant Engineer United States Navy, Commanding.

STAFF.

George DeForest Barton, Paymaster United States Navy.
Francis B. Allen, Second Assistant Engineer United States Navy.
Aaron Vanderbilt, Acting Ensign United States Navy.
J. Homer Darling, Actg. Asst. Surgeon.
Capt. Chas. H. Townshend.
T. H. Thorne, Actg. Paymaster, United States Navy.

Navy Drum Corps of New Haven.

Band or other Music from Men-of-War in Harbor.

Battery of Howitzers, and a Battalion of 500 Sailors and Marines from U. S. Steamers " Richmond," " Galena " and " Yantic."

Admiral David D. Porter, Rear Admiral, S. T. Luce, Commanding United States Naval Force, North Atlantic Station, Admiral J. W. A. Nicholson, and the following Commanders of vessels in the harbor: Capt. Robt. Boyd, U. S. N., Commander ; Colly M. Chester, U. S. N., Commander, Francis M. Green, U. S. N., Captain Augustus R. S. Foote, Lieutenant Loyal Farragut, in carriages.

Model of U. S. Frigate " Constitution," loaned by the New Haven Colony Historical Society.

Mexican Veterans in carriages.

Landrigan's Band, of New Haven.

NAVAL VETERAN ASSOCIATION

OF CONNECTICUT.

Captain Charles A. Stillman, United States Marine Corps, Commanding.

STAFF.

S. P. Crafts, Acting Volunteer Lieutenant United States Navy.

William C. Staples, Acting Master United States Navy.

F. H. Grannis, Assistant Surgeon United States Navy.

S. W. Adams, Assistant Paymaster.

L. D. White, Treas. Navy Vet. Association.

S. G. Slaters, Actg. Vol. Lieut., U. S. N.

G. H. Prescott, Actg. Ensign.

Chas. H. Lester, Actg. Ensign.

First Co., Capt. J. C. Jackson.

Second Co., Capt. E. Hubbell.

Third Co., Capt. Carlos Babcock.

Fourth Co., Capt. E. T. Rancor.

Fifth Co., Capt. E. Dillon.

One-fifth Size Model of the original " Monitor " that defeated the Confederate steamer " Merrimac " at Hampton Roads, Va., March 9, 1862.

SONS OF VETERANS,

CONNECTICUT DIVISION.

Clinton Brass Band.

Lieutenant-Colonel Charles K. Farnham, New Haven, Commanding.
Major George Warren, Jr., Putnam.
Adjutant A. E. Penfield.
Quartermaster G. Brainard Smith, Hartford.
Judge Advocate F. J. Linsley.

Nathan Hale Camp No. 1, New Haven, Captain F. J. Allard.
Buckingham Camp No. 3. Norwich, Captain J. L. Kingsley.
T. E. Hawley Camp No. 4, Forestville. Captain H. McGar.
J. R. Hawley Camp No. 5, Guilford, Captain J. F. Wildman.
Griffin A. Stedman Camp No. 6, Hartford, Captain J. Fred Burpee.
C. L. Upham Camp No. 7, Meriden, Captain W. E. Lewis.
G. S. Wyant Camp No. 8, Seymour, Captain W. S. Healey.
Chatfield Camp No. 9. Waterbury, Captain F. W. Ingraham.
N. L. White Camp No. 10, Danbury, Captain T. H. Holdinst.
William H. Mallory Camp No. 11, Bridgeport, Captain C. C. Wilson.
E. W. Gibbons Camp No. 13, Middletown, Captain G. A. Southmayd.
B. F. Fitch Camp No. 14, South Norwalk, Captain W. B. Kendrick.
Platt Camp No. 15, Westbrook, Captain C. A. Grosvenor.
F. S. Seymour Camp No. 16, New Britain, Captain A. S. Maguess.
Wright Camp No. 17, Thomaston, Captain Wallace Fisher.
M. I. Tourtellotte Camp No. 18, Putnam, Captain George Warren, Jr.
Albert Latham Camp No. 19, Mystic Bridge, Captain E. E. Latham.
John A. Tibbitts Camp No. 20, New London, Captain R. Mussell.
S. S. Woodruff Camp No. 21, Southington, Captain C. W. Dutton.
T. B. Robinson Camp No. 22, Bristol, Captain M. A. Bennett.
C. D. Blinn Camp No. 23, New Milford, Captain F. S. Gregory.
Nathaniel Lyon Camp No. 24, Danielsonville, Captain Walter E. Kies.
W. B. Wooster Camp No. 25, Ansonia, Captain E. H. Tomlinson.
C. L. Russell Camp No. 26, Birmingham, Captain A. J. Ewen.
John F. Carroll Camp No. 27, East Hartford, Captain Charles E. Tryon.
John A. Logan Camp No. 28, South Windham, Captain P. E. Bowen.
S. B. Horne Camp No. 29, Winsted, Captain H. M. Eddy.

THIRD DIVISION.

NATIONAL AND MEMORIAL.

The unbroken Sisterhood of States, represented by young ladies from the Sunday Schools, escorted by the Public School Memorial Guard.

Brevet Brigadier-General, Rev. Erastus Blakeslee, Marshal.

ASSISTANT MARSHALS.

Major Ruel P. Cowles.
Captain Charles J. Buckbee, Sixth Connecticut Volunteers.
Lieutenant Charles B. Dyer, First Connecticut Cavalry Volunteers.
John L. Saxe, Fourth New York Cavalry Volunteers.
Rev. J. E. Twitchell, D.D., Chaplain 131st Ohio Volunteers.
Rev. I. M. Foster, Private 146th New York Volunteers, and Past Chaplain-in-
Chief. G. A. R.
Rev. S. H. Bray.
Rev. P. S. Evans, Chaplain Thirteenth New York Heavy Artillery.
Mr. John C. North.

FIRST SECTION.—ESCORT.

Capt. Benjamin Jepson, Assistant Marshal, Commanding.

Meriden City Band, Walter Phœnix, Leader.

PUBLIC SCHOOL MEMORIAL GUARD, NEW HAVEN, CONN.

Battalion Drum Corps.

FIELD AND STAFF.

Acting Colonel, Assistant Marshal Capt. Benj. Jepson.
Acting Lieutenant Colonel, Assistant Marshal Lieut. Henry W. Loomis.
Acting Major, Assistant Marshal Captain William G. Dickinson.
Acting Adjutant, Arthur W. Jepson.
Quartermaster, George H. Leopold.
Paymaster, Winfield P. Dann.
Surgeon, Wilbur L. Chamberlain.
Assistant Surgeon, Harry R. Northrop.
Signal Officer, F. H. Stevens.
Inspector, George N. Shiner.
Sergeant Major, Wm. Keegan.
Quartermaster Sergeant, Frank B. Harris.
Commissary Sergeant, Arthur Smith.
Hospital Steward, Fred. H. Beard.
Drum Major, Herman Hendricks.

HIGH SCHOOL COMPANY (58 Boys)—Capt. Frederick Frost.
1st Lieut. Arthur Moody; 2d Lieut. James Earle; 3d Lieut. Frank
White; Standard Bearer, George Hart.

EATON COMPANY (58 Boys)—Capt. Charles Bassett.
1st Lieut. Arthur Foote; 2d Lieut. Isaac Heller; 3d Lieut. Edward Uhl;
Standard Bearer, George Johnson.

DWIGHT COMPANY (58 Boys)—Capt. Jerome Donovan.
1st Lieut. M. Alling; 2d Lieut. Wallace Curtis; 3d Lieut. Joseph Ward;
Standard Bearer, Harry Holcomb.

WASHINGTON COMPANY (58 Boys)—Capt. William Fisher.
1st Lieut. Victor Koweleski; 2d Lieut. Frank Hoyt; 3d Lieut. Riley
Phillips; Standard Bearer, Albert Hall.

HAMILTON COMPANY (58 Boys)—Capt. John Rodigan.
1st Lieut. Lawrence Cashman; 2d Lieut. James Moakley; 2d Lieut.
James Kehoe; Standard Bearer, Willie Farrell.

WELCH (COLOR) COMPANY (58 Boys)—Capt. Howard Embler.
1st Lieut. C. Somers; 2d Lieut. H. Lewis; 3d Lieut. R. Billings;
Standard Bearer, J. Faulhaber.

WINCHESTER COMPANY (58 Boys)—Capt. Walter Frey.
1st Lieut. William Gobelin; 2d Lieut. Fred. Bitz; 3d Lieut. August
Strible; Standard Bearer, Cleaveland Walker.

WOOLSEY COMPANY (58 Boys)—Capt. Van Buren Lamb.
  1st Lieut. Edward Morgan; 2d Lieut. Fred. Williams; 3d Lieut. James
  E. Smith; Standard Bearer, Robert Scranton.

SKINNER COMPANY (58 Boys)—Capt. Joseph Johnson.
  1st Lieut. William Beers; 2d Lieut. Henry Brewer; 3d Lieut. Phillip
  Farnsworth; Standard Bearer, James Smith.

WOOSTER COMPANY (58 Boys)—Capt. Ralph True.
  1st Lieut. George Seward; 2d Lieut. Robert Devine; 3d Lieut. Fred.
  Hollis; Standard Bearer, William Gardner.

WEBSTER COMPANY (58 Boys)—Capt. Sim Embler.
  1st Lieut. W. Phelps; 2d Lieut. A. Richter; 3d Lieut. J. Walter;
  Standard Bearer, H. Chapman.

SECOND SECTION.—BARGES REPRESENTING STATES.

H. P. Hubbard, Assistant Marshal, Commanding.

ASSISTANT MARSHALS.

Col. Henry R. Loomis.   Fred. A. Betts.
Horace P. Shares.   Charles F. Hubbard.

New Britain City Band, William H. Sperry, Leader.

Thirty-eight Decorated Barges, representing the States of the Union; and
occupied by delegations of young ladies from fifty-two Sunday Schools: the
first thirteen states in the order of their adoption of the Constitution, and the
others in the order of their admission, as follows, viz;

Oscar J. Hull, Assistant Marshal.

1. Delaware, December 7, 1787.—Barge "Leader," containing thirty young
    ladies from Second Congregational Sunday School, Fair Haven.

Wm. F. Norman, Assistant Marshal.

2. Pennsylvania, December 12, 1787.—Float "Liberty," containing twenty-
    six young ladies from First Baptist Sunday School and Nash Street
    Mission Sunday School.

3. New Jersey, December 18, 1787.—Barge "Monmouth," containing fourteen young ladies from East Pearl Street Methodist Episcopal Sunday School.

J. Edward Judson, Assistant Marshal.

4. Georgia, January 2, 1788.—Barge "Rock Wagon," containing twelve young ladies from Ferry Street Congregational Sunday School.

5. Connecticut, January 9, 1788.—Barge "Wanderer," containing sixteen young ladies from Center Church Sunday School and Lebanon Mission.

John H. Connor, Assistant Marshal.

6. Massachusetts, February 16, 1788.—Boat "Mayflower," containing group of Pilgrims and twenty little children representing all nations, from Church of Messiah Sunday School.

7. Maryland, April 28, 1788.—Barge "Pioneer," containing twenty young ladies from Sacred Heart and St. John's R. C. Sunday Schools.

John T. Doyle, Assistant Marshal.

8. South Carolina, May 23, 1788.—Barge "Campus," containing twenty-eight young ladies from Taylor and Summerfield Sunday Schools.

9. New Hampshire, June 21, 1788.—Barge "Wooding, Jr.," containing twenty young ladies from Trinity Methodist Sunday School.

Edward I. Atwater, Assistant Marshal.

10. New York, June 26, 1788.—Barge "Nightingale" of Wallingford, containing twenty-six young ladies from Trinity Church Sunday School and Mission.

11. Virginia, June 26, 1788.—Float, containing sixteen young ladies from Church of the Redeemer Sunday School.

Capt. Lawrence O'Brien, Assistant Marshal.

12. North Carolina, November 21, 1789.—Barge "Columbia," containing thirty girls from the New Haven Orphan Asylum.

13. Rhode Island, May 29, 1790.—Barge "City of Rome," containing eighteen young ladies from Calvary Baptist Sunday School.

J. D. Bradley, Assistant Marshal.

14. Vermont, March 4, 1791. — Barge "Taurus," containing fourteen young ladies from College Street Sunday School.

15. Kentucky, February 4, 1792.—Barge " Yale," containing thirty young ladies from St. James and Grace Sunday Schools.

Elliott H. Morse, Assistant Marshal.

16. Tennessee, June 1, 1796.—Barge " Wallingford," containing twenty-eight young ladies from Third M. E. and German M. E. Sunday Schools.

17. Ohio, November 29, 1802.—Barge " Quinnipiac," containing sixteen young ladies from First Congregational Sunday School, Fair Haven.

Fred H. Benton, Assistant Marshal.

18. Louisiana, April 8, 1812.—Barge " Lewis, Jr.," containing sixteen young ladies from the Dwight Place Sunday School.

19. Indiana, December 11, 1816.—Barge " Nesbitt," containing twenty-eight young ladies from the Westville Sunday Schools.

Salmon G. Pease, Assistant Marshal.

20. Mississippi, December 10, 1817.—Barge " East Shore," containing twenty-eight young ladies from Emanuel Baptist Sunday School.

21. Illinois, December 3, 1818.—Barge "City of Elms," containing thirty young ladies from English Hall Sunday School.

Harry Morell, Assistant Marshal.

22. Alabama, December 14th, 1819.—Barge " West Shore," containing thirty young ladies from the Sunday Schools of Church of Ascension and All Saints' Mission.

23. Maine, March 15, 1820.—Barge " Transit," containing twenty young ladies from the United Church Sunday School.

A. M. Loomis, Assistant Marshal.

24. Missouri, March 3d, 1821.—Barge " Davis No. 32," containing twenty young ladies from Mishkan Israel and Benai Scholom Sunday Schools.

25. Arkansas, June 15th, 1836.—Barge " Venus," containing sixteen young ladies from St. Mary's Sunday School.

William E. Perry, Assistant Marshal.

26. Michigan, January 26, 1837.—Barge " Davis No. 12," containing thirteen young ladies from the St. John's Episcopal Sunday School.

27. Florida, March 23d, 1845.—Barge "Saltonstall," containing twenty-eight young ladies from Humphrey Street Sunday School.

Capt. Jason D. Thompson, Assistant Marshal.

28. Texas, December 24th, 1845.—Boat "Lone Star," containing twenty-three young ladies from West Haven Sunday Schools.

29. Iowa, December 28th, 1846.—Barge "Gypsey," containing twenty-four young ladies from First Methodist Sunday School.

Frederick Ley, Assistant Marshal.

30. Wisconsin, May 29th, 1848.—Barge "America," containing thirty young ladies from St. Patrick's Sunday School.

31. California, September 9th, 1850.—Barge "Rambler," containing sixteen young ladies from the Grand avenue Baptist Sunday School.

A. M. Hiller, Assistant Marshal.

32. Minnesota, May 11, 1858.—Barge "Carryall," containing twenty-eight young ladies from the German Baptist Sunday School and Mission.

33. Oregon, February 14, 1859.—Barge "Daisy," containing sixteen young ladies from St. John St. M. E. Sunday School.

Albert M. Bartlett, Assistant Marshal.

34. Kansas, January 29, 1861.—Barge "Wooding, Sr.," containing twenty-six young ladies from the Dixwell avenue Congregational Sunday School.

35. West Virginia, December 31, 1863.—Barge "Fort Hale," containing twenty-eight young ladies from the Sunday Schools at
Four Corners and Morris Cove.

W. E. Whittlesey, Assistant Marshal.

36. Nevada, March 21, 1864.—Barge "Regicide," containing thirty young ladies from Howard Avenue Congregational and
Baptist Mission Sunday Schools.

37. Nebraska, March 1, 1867.—Barge "Florence," containing fourteen young ladies from St. Boniface Sunday School.

Lieut. Arthur M. Howarth, Assistant Marshal.

38. Colorado, March 3, 1875.—Barge "Nightingale," containing thirty young ladies from St. Paul's and St. Thomas' Sunday Schools.

FOURTH DIVISION.

UNIFORMED CIVIC SOCIETIES.

Marshal—Major Charles W. Blakeslee, Jr.

ASSISTANT MARSHALS.

Major George H. Larned, Major Theron A. Todd. Captain Rollin C. Newton,
Horace B. Perry, Henry W. Sanford, J. Samuel Scranton,
N. Albert Hooker, Dwight W. Blakeslee.
H. N. Whittlesey, John H. Phillips.

Tingue Band, of Seymour.

Colonel E. F. Durand and Staff.

KNIGHTS OF PYTHIAS.

DIVISION NO. 1.—Captain George A. Cornell.
DIVISION Nos. 2 and 3.—Captain John H. Norman.
DIVISION No. 4.—Captain T. M. Smith.

Colonel P. P. Thomas and Staff, New York.

First Regiment Uniformed Rank, Knights of Pythias, New York.

Sarsfield Zouaves, Capt. Albert Tanyan.

IN CARRIAGES.

L. D. Chidsey, Assistant Marshal.

Mayor S. A. York, of New Haven, and visiting Mayors of other cities.
Ex-Mayors of New Haven.
Town Agent and Selectmen, of New Haven and visiting Selectmen of other towns.
Board of Aldermen and Councilmen of the City of New Haven.
Ex-Governors of Connecticut.
Judges of United States and State Courts.
Speaker of House of Representatives.
Ex-Congressmen of State of Connecticut and other invited guests.
Ex-Governor A. H. Holley.
Ex-Governor W. T. Miner.
Ex-Governor Charles B. Andrews.
Hon. J. D. Park.
Hon. Dwight Loomis.
Hon. Elisha Carpenter.
Hon. H. W. R. Hoyt.
Hon. E. J. Doolittle.
Hon. H. E. Benton.
Hon. Benjamin Douglass.
Hon. George M. Landers.
Hon. Jeremiah Olney.
Hon. Charles J. Hoadley.
Hon. Thomas W. Williams.
Hon. E. S. Cleveland.
Hon. J. R. Buck.
Hon. S. W. Kellogg.
Hon. Stiles T. Stanton.
Hon. Henry C. Robinson.
Hon. Nathaniel Shipman.
Lewis E. Stanton.
William H. Maynard.
James P. Platt.
Robert O. Gates.
Richard C. Morris.
Miles B. Preston.
Henry P. Burr.
Edwin Andrews.

George W. Tingley.
John B. Mix.
H. B. Steele.
Charles D. Perkins.
George Watson.
W. P. Adams.
Alex. Boyle.
Herbert C. Peters.
And other guests.

MAYORS.

Hon. A. Bentley, New Britain.
Hon. George F. Tinker, New London.
Hon. H. S. Boughton, Waterbury.
Hon Hugh O'Brien, Boston.
Hon. C. H. S. Davis, Meriden.
Hon. C. R. Woodward, Middletown.
Hon. Theophilis Oiena, Brooklyn.
Hon. C. Fones, Bridgeport.
Hon. E. B. Maynard, Springfield.
Hon. M. G. Bulkley, Hartford.
Hon. Jos. E. Haynes, Newark.
Hon. W. B. Hubbard, Norwalk.

HAMMONASSETT TRIBE RED MEN, NEW HAVEN.

J. E. Hunt, Sachem; J. W. Hatstatt, Senior Sagamore; A. L. Hill, Junior Sagamore; Carlos Smith, Prophet.

FIFTH DIVISION.

Marshal—Charles Weidig.

ASSISTANT MARSHALS.

H. Hessler, J. B. Richards, George Rotman, John Guyer, Leopold Herz,
N. Heiler, J. Warrenberger, Augustus Kapitzky, S. Beck, Henry
Weideman, Augustus Reisinger, A. F. Kusterers, Jacob
Broschart, Charles Schenck, E. Krause.

Stamford Band.

Turner Society, James Petts.

Arion Singing Society, William Dahlmeyer.

Harugari Singing Society, Bartholomew Weeks.

Teutonia Singing Society, William Kusterer.

Cecilia Singing Society, Frank Dahlmeyer.

Bavarian Society, Phillip Hugo.

Hessen Society, Mich. Hessler.

Schwaben Society, Jacob Warrenberger.

Plattdeutsche Society, Ernest Klenke.

Viking Swedish Society, Barry Holm.

40

SIXTH DIVISION.

CIVIC SOCIETIES.

Major William A. Lincoln, Marshal.

ASSISTANT MARSHALS.

James P. Bree, Adjutant.
Major Hiram Camp.
Major Joseph H. Keefe.
Major R. A. Belden,
Michael Dillon.
J. J. Brennan.
Patrick Doyle.
B. J. Dillon.
W. O. Staples.
Capt. R. J. Bunce.
W. H. Fitzgerald.
Dr. J. M. Reilly.
Capt. P. O'Connor.
Peter Carberry.
Joseph R. Manning.

F. H. Savage,
Dennis Keane.
Thos. Leddy.
Jos. O'Gorman.
J. Edward Geary.
T. F. McGuinness.
T. F. McGrail.
John H. Dillon.
Dr. M. C. O'Connar.
Alex. McDonald.
P. McGuinness.
John D. Cunningham.
James Connors.
James Cavanaugh.
Capt. J. H. Pettis.

Portchester Cornet Band, C. Blaney, Leader.
Vol. Veteran Fireman's Association, New Haven, Charles Doty, Foreman;
Benjamin F. Brockett, Assistant Foreman.
Winchester Hose Co., New Haven, Walter Hurlburt Foreman, Henry
Hamilton, Assistant Foreman.
Santa Maria Council, No. 8, Knights of Columbus, Dennis Nolan.
San Salvador Council, No. 1, Knights of Columbus, J. F. Galvin.
Knights of St. Patrick, Frank E. Craig, Prest.

41

PATRIOTIC SONS OF AMERICA.

Washington Camp No. 1, C. A. Ross.
"   "   "   2, H. H. Haydon.
"   "   "   3, H H. Denton.
"   "   "   4, J. H. Flagg.

ORDER OF UNITED AMERICAN MECHANICS.

Pioneer Council No. 1, E. E. Stevens.
Washington Council No. 2, F. Brown.
Garfield Council, No. 14, G. E. Parker.

SONS OF TEMPERANCE.

Harmony Division No 5, Charles E. Hart.
Crystal Wave Division No. 7, W. W. Johnson.
Fair Haven Division No. 36, W. H. Richards.

SOCIETY FRATELLANZA ITALIANA.

ASSISTANT MARSHALS.

Charles Arienta.
Eugene Delgrago.
John Sella.
Nichola Murana.
Fratellanza Italiana Society, Autony D. Matty, President, Paul Russo, Marshal.
Garibaldi Society, L. D. Bella.
And others.

SEVENTH DIVISION.

NEW HAVEN FIRE DEPARTMENT.

Tubb's Military Band, Norwich.

Marshal—Lieutenant Colonel A. C. Hendrick, Chief Fire Department.

ASSISTANT MARSHALS.

Assistant Chief, Andrew Kennedy; Assistant Chief, William C. Smith; Assistant Chief, John L. Disbrow.

STEAM FIRE ENGINE COMPANY No. 1.—Capt. Edward I. Barrett.
STEAM FIRE ENGINE COMPANY No. 2.—Capt. William H. Hubbard.
STEAM FIRE ENGINE COMPANY No. 3.—Capt. Charles B. Dyer.
STEAM FIRE ENGINE COMPANY No. 4.—Capt. Christopher L. Langley.
HOOK AND LADDER COMPANY No. 1.—Capt. Charles H. Hilton.
STEAM FIRE ENGINE COMPANY No. 5.—Capt. Henry Tuttle.
STEAM FIRE ENGINE COMPANY No. 6.—Capt. Wilfred H. Spang.
HOSE COMPANY No. 7.—Capt. John W. Stoddard.
STEAM FIRE ENGINE COMPANY No. 8.—Capt. James J. Bradnack.
HOOK AND LADDER COMPANY No. 3.—Capt. Henry J. Wilson.

By order of GENERAL EDWIN S. GREELEY,
Grand Marshal.

JOHN G. HEALY,

OFFICIAL: Lt.-Col. and Adj.-General.

FRED. H. WALDRON,
Capt. and Asst. Adjt.-General.

EXERCISES AT THE MONUMENT.

As the escort appears in sight of the Park, a salute of seventeen guns will be fired from Indian Head. Upon reaching the summit of East Rock where the monument stands the following dedication exercises will take place:

Opening Address,   Timothy Dwight, D.D., L. L. D.
President of Yale College.

2. National Anthem " America," by grand chorus of Memorial Guard, under direction of Professor Jepson.

3. Invocation, by Rev. Edwin Harwood, D. D.

4. Song, German societies, " This is the Day of the Lord."

5. Unveiling of the Monument by Comrades George W. Warner, Post 17 ; Almarine Hayward, Post 52 ; Wiegand Schlein, Post 76, and Veteran Sailor Capt. H. P. Crafts.

Oration,   Rev. Newman Smyth, D.D.

7. The surrender of the Monument to the town by General S. E. Merwin, representing Monument Committee.

8. Acceptance of the Monument by the town—Selectman Louis Feldman.

9. Song—The Red, White and Blue, by the Memorial Guard.

10. The town presenting the Monument to the city by First Selectman James Reynolds.

11. Accepting the trust by Mayor York.

12. Floral decoration of the Monument by the young ladies representing the States.

13. Unfurling of the City Flag by the Mayor.

14.   Unfurling of the State Flag by the Governor.

15.   Unfurling of the National Flag by General Fairchild, commander-in-chief of the Grand Army.

16.   Song—The Star Spangled Banner, by the grand chorus of Memorial Guard, accompanied by the bands ; salute from artillery on Snake Rock and war vessels in the harbor.

17.   Return march of military and other organizations to the city escorting the guests.

AFTERNOON.

4 o'clock—Band Concert on the Green by Tubb's Military Band of Norwich.

4.30 o'clock—Exhibition of Day Fireworks from the plain at the base of East Rock.

AT SUNSET.

The bells will be rung and national salute fired.

EVENING.

At 8 o'clock the Second Regiment Band will give a concert on the Green, and at 8.30 there will be the following brilliant display of

FIREWORKS.

The signal for the commencement of the display will be a heavy petard shell. This will be followed by a grand illumination of the assembled multitude and all surrounding objects by crimson fires of intense reflective power.

1.   Lighted Shell.
2.   Grand illumination.
3.   Discharge of shells.
4.   Display of Asteroid rockets.
5.   Welcome.   The motto " Welcome."
6.   Discharge of Japanese umbrella wheels.
7.   Display of heavy minnie shells.
8.   Device, wheel of Prometheus.
9.   Display of rockets.
10.   Discharge of heavy bombs.

45

11. Set piece, the Concord minute man. Emblematic of the struggle for independence.

12. Discharge of heavy rockets with garniture of driven and duration stars.

13. Display of bombs with Japanese golden or trailing stars of beautiful effect.

14. The constellation Pleiades.

15. Golden fountain arranged in pyramidal form and displaying far-reaching and powerful jets of sparkling light.

16. Discharge of whirling dragon wheels rising in succession from the ground.

17. "Our Heroes."

18. Display of heavy shells with Union stars in red, white and blue

19. Parachute rockets of the heaviest calibre.

20. Device, In Memoriam. The American shield in red, white and blue lance with jets and halos of spun fire, surmounts the name of New Haven's gallant son, Colonel Henry C. Merwin, beneath which is shown in brilliant colors the name of the battle in which he fell (Gettysburg).

21. Grand line of batteries extending across the entire green.

22. Discharge of heavy mines with streamers and lilac and ruby stars.

23. Device in honor of Rear Admiral Foote. The name of New Haven's gallant sailor in letters of colored lance is surmounted by the Rear Admiral's flag, surrounded by halos of sun fire, while beneath blazes the name of his most signal victory, "Donelson." The device is terminated by a gun salute with petards.

24. Grand flight of silver sancissions thrown en masse from a single point, each ending with loud explosion.

25. Display of heavy asteroid rockets with floating jewels of flashing and changing colors.

26. Sunburst.

27. Discharge of bombs with garniture of twinkling will-o'-the-wisp stars.

28. Chinese meteors rising and falling with eccentric motion, each with brilliant halos of golden spur fire.

29. Device in honor of General A. H. Terry. The name of the general in colored lance fires supporting the American flag in red, white and blue ; beneath appears the name of his great battle in support of the Union. "Fort Fisher." An artillery salute terminates the piece.

30. Flight of golden comets with fiery tails, dropping jewels in both ascent and descent.

31. Discharge of mammoth bombs showing great clouds of golden rain and Japanese tailed stars.

32. Devise See Saw ; the old nursery rhyme pyrotechnically illustrated with comic termination.

33. Discharge of large asteroid rockets with penchant flashing jewels of emerald and ruby flame.

34. Heavy mine display with parti-colored stars and showers of spur fire.

35. Set piece, the soldier of the republic. A full-sized figure of a soldier of the Union army supporting the American flag draped gracefully about its staff while the sword is grasped in readiness for the defense of the banner.

36. Grand flight of shells thrown simultaneously from a single point bursting in mid-air.

37. Display of golden fountains arranged in pyramidal form, each with far-reaching jets of dazzling brilliant fire.

38. Set piece, Serpent and Butterfly.

39. Aerial wheels revolving horizontally and rising and falling with showers of golden rain.

40. Display of rockets with garniture of stars of extreme beauty.

41. Device. "The Monitor." A representation in silver fire of the monitor arched with the name of "Bushnell," New Haven's citizen to whom was due the honor of its appearance at a most critical moment; the whole rests upon the name of the inventor, Erickson. Grand halos surround the whole and heavy and repeated petard explosions terminate the piece.

42. Discharge of parachute rockets, detaching floating crimson and azure stars.

43. Grand illumination with India and Chinese colored fires.

44. Device, Peace and Plenty.

47

45. Discharge of mammoth bombs with showers of driven and duration stars.

46. Display of rockets with golden rain.

47. A representation of the American flag in red, white and blue, surrounded by the words: Port Hudson, Fredericksburg, Gettysburg, Antietam and Appomattox.

48. Discharge of tourbillons fired in masses, each with circlets of golden flame.

49. Grand line of batteries discharging amid repeated and heavy explosions.

50. Set piece, Falls of Niagara.

51. Grand flight of silver saucissons, each with one cometic silver tail and termination in petard explosion.

52. Discharge of heavy shells with double brilliant golden meteors.

53. Display of rockets with garniture of national colors.

54. Grand Army badge.

55. Flight of silver comets rising with brilliant tails and eccentric motion to a great height when they terminate with heavy explosions.

56. Grand line of Chinese aerial wheels of golden flames and jets and rays of star fire.

57. Discharge of mines with masses of ruby, emerald, topaz and amethyst jeweled points.

58. Display of towering rockets with great variety of garniture.

59. Final grand illumination with India and Chinese colored fires of intense reflective powers.

60. Grand finale. In the center towers high in the air a representation in silver lance of the soldiers monument, flanked on either side by three elaborate columns, each bearing the names of the New England States. Between the columns are shown banners each with a badge of one of the G. A. R. corps. The entire device is over-arched at the close by an immense bouquet of 400 rockets discharged simultaneously, filling the air with myriads of stars of every hue and color together with great showers of gold rain, spur and bee fire.

COMMITTEES.

Committee on Soldiers' Monument, S. E. Merwin, Chairman; Simeon J. Fox, Secretary; James E. English, H. B. Bigelow, H. B. Harrison, John F. Weir, James Reynolds, Theo. A. Tuttle, J. D. Plunkett, John McCarthy, John G. Healy, Conrad Hofacker, Samuel Tolles Frank D. Sloat.

Executive Committee, S. A. York, James Reynolds, S. E. Merwin.

Committee on Finance, N. D. Sperry, Chairman; B. R. English, Treasurer.
Committee on Invitations, S. A. York, Chairman.
Committee on Literary Exercises, H. B. Harrison, Chairman.
Committee on Citizens' Reception, S. A. York, Chairman.
Committee on Military Reception, S. R. Smith, Chairman.
Committee on Grand Army Reception, James N. Coe, Chairman.
Committee on Salutes and Bells, William A. Lincoln, Chairman.
Committee on Instrumental Music, A. C. Hendrick, Chairman.
Committee on Printing, Eli Whitney, Jr., Chairman.
Committee on Order of Exercises, J. D. Plunkett, Chairman.
Committee on Transportation, W. S. Wells, Chairman.
Committee on Civic Societies, Carlos Smith, Chairman.
Committee on Sunday Schools, Rev. Erastus Blakeslee, Chairman.
Committee on Public Schools, S. T. Dutton, Chairman.
Committee on Vocal Music, Benjamin Jepson, Chairman.
Committee on Decorations, H. P. Hubbard, Chairman.
Committee on Fireworks, F. A. Munson, Chairman.
Committee on Carriages, W. J. Atwater, Chairman.
Committee on Refreshments, J. Rice Winchell, Chairman.
Committee on Grand Stand, Noyes E. Edwards, Chairman.
Committee on Chief Marshal and Assistants, C. F. Bollman, Chairman
Committee on Fire Department, James T. Mullen, Chairman
Committee on Press Reception, F. M. Lovejoy, Chairman.
Committee on Ice Water, H. L. Dorman, Chairman

John E. Earle, Chairman Special Committee on Reception.
Samuel A. York, Chairman General Committee.
Samuel E. Merwin, Vice-Chairman General Committee.
Simeon J. Fox, Secretary General Committee.
Benjamin R. English, Treasurer General Committee.

A. H. KELLAM,
Secretary Sub-Committee

www.ingramcontent.com/pod-product-compliance
Lightning Source LLC
Chambersburg PA
CBHW021433090426
42739CB00009B/1470